Dedicated to the author's inspirations.

M.D. Tophus

Trauma United, Life Defined. A Healthcare Tool for Professionals Across the Globe.

Copyright ©. 2022. M.D. Tophus. All rights reserved.

Hilphma Publications 2022. www.hilphmapublication.com

First Edition.

Germany.

The content provided herein is for educational purposes. No liability is assumed for losses or damages due to the information provided. Any resemblance to actual persons, living or dead, businesses, companies, events or locations is entirely coincidental.

The author has over 25 years of clinical experience in the healthcare field. Is cognisant of both DSM-5-TR (and previous versions) and ICD-11 (and previous versions) disorders and conditions; quality and safety improvement in healthcare; and healthcare education.

Emotions may be expressed culturally differently but at its core the same emotions (both negative and positive) are experienced similarly the world over.

Likewise, the emotional content expressed from traumatic experiences. Some populations may be taught more readily to suppress them, leave the reactions to later (and certainly in the case of ongoing conflict, or ongoing trauma, this becomes a necessity along with the natural adrenaline which places them in a fight or flight state at that present time).

Others may be taught (often depending upon gender) to repress the trauma responses and attempt to overcome them, for instance, for the sake of 'manhood'.

Nevertheless, the internal workings of a person can never lie, delude, or spontaneously forget.

Where there is suppression and repression of such emotions, the trauma symptoms invariably emerge and emanate via unique and often unpredictable ways.

It can range from new insidious habits and behaviors through to outright rage, mental instability, and semi-permanent (to permanent) cognitive and personality changes.

Accordingly, *a witness to the trauma, and the impact of the primary trauma (and traumatised) upon family members, carers, friends, key healthcare and other workers, often have consequences beyond the shedding of a single tear.*

This publication deals specifically with: Complex Post-Traumatic Stress Disorder (CPTSD); health Care providers' Second Victim Syndrome (SVS); Post-Traumatic Stress Disorder (PTSD); and Acute Stress Disorder (ASD).

That is, from diagnosis through to assessment, treatment, risk, resource and support accessability, worst case situations, and the involvement of police, and emergency personnel.

D.V; Sexual Assault; Gang violence; Medical error and Critical incidents, are just some of the topics for examination in the assessment section of this publication.

The author has remained mindful of the various healthcare professions involved in assisting/diagnosing trauma victims, this includes Physicians through to allied healthcare staff, and beyond. Thus the assessment, treatment, and related information is kept contextually relevant in this regard.

It also incorporates some culturally diverse aspects.

Other M.D. Tophus publications available:

"Exercising Quality in Healthcare Service Provision: A Complex Care Workbook for All Healthcare Professionals." Hilphma Publications: 2022.

"Who is This Colleague?: Dangers of the Healthcare Profession, and beyond. An Interview Guide for Recruitment, Performance Appraisal and Post-Adverse Events."
Hilphma Publications: 2022.

"Think on your Feet: Those Who Can. For the Consummate Healthcare Professional."
Hilphma Publications: 2022.

"The Unfortunate Healthcare Treater, The Hapless Healthcare Therapist: Narcissistic and Borderline Personality Disorder clients. The Grit."
Hilphma Publications: 2022.

"Victims of Crime: Introduction to Forensic Challenges in Healthcare."
Hilphma Publications: 2022.

"The A to Z of Workplace Bullying: For the Healthcare Professional and Beyond."
Hilphma Publications: 2022.

CONTENTS

This publication is written as a guide only. There are numerous different diagnostic measures, assessments, and treatments, which exist.

Often, the assessor- treater has preferred methods and procedures to which they adhere, for multiple reasons.

For those readers to whom that applies, discussion of the provided information becomes part of the process of deliberation in preparation for the post-assessment section, the risks, and the resource acquisition and necessities.

The content featured in the following pages, however, incorporates mainstream approaches of the seasoned healthcare provider.

ASD: ACUTE STRESS DISORDER

ASD is commonly known as *psychological shock.*

Duration of symptoms: *3 days to 1 month* time frame following a traumatic incident/s.

Can be *delayed symptomatology* before onset.

DSM-5-TR criteria:

Development of the disorder by "exposure to actual or threatened death, serious injury, or sexual violence"(1). It extends to having witnessed the event; gaining information about a loved one having suffered (in reference to the above quote); or repeated exposure to details of events involving trauma.

Physical symptoms: heart palpitations, breathing difficulty; perspiring alot; hypervigilance; insomnia; exaggerated startle response; physical (or verbal) aggression.

Psychological symptoms: trauma specific dreams; intrusive trauma memories; flashbacks; significant and lengthy psychological suffering regarding the traumatic incident/s; negative mood; dissociative symptoms; avoidance of triggers; arousal symptoms; memories of the incident/s.

Historical trauma can predispose to ASD.

Seems to be more prevalent in *females*.

Early diagnosis can reduce symptom severity and reduce chance of developing *PTSD*.

Differential diagnosis: adjustment disorder, though usually not triggered by a life/death/ perilous event and usually presents with less physiological reactions (heart pounding etc).

NB: 'Acute Stress Reaction' is not included in ICD-11 (though it was in the ICD-10).

PTSD: Post-Traumatic Stress Disorder

With regard to, **DSM-5-TR** criteria:

Much of the Acute Stress Disorder criteria above pertains also to PTSD.
With both ASD and PTSD, the criteria also includes individuals (eg **emergency services, police**) who are repeatedly exposed to "aversive details of the traumatic event" (1).

Duration of symptoms: **beyond 1 month** time frame.

Dissociative symptoms are categorized in one of 2 ways: depersonalization (detachment); or, derealization (synonymous with a dream-like state).

The **ICD-11** criteria is summarised as:

"Exposure to an extremely threatening or horrific event or series of events" (2).

Duration of symptoms: at the least for **several weeks**.

There must be **significant impact (or impairment)** on one or more areas of life functioning.

Primary symptom indicators: "re-experiencing", "avoidance", "persistent perceptions of heightened current threat" (2).

Historically:

PTSD "..was first conceptualized- as "Nostalgia" in the mid-1700s and the more commonly known term "Shell Shock" in the early 1900s" (3).

It can be triggered by "Medical conditions such as cancer, facial disfiguration, and limb amputation" (3).

India, for example- the symptom of 'avoidance' (in thinking about/talking about the traumatic incident/s) within PTSD- are incidentally lower (3).

Culturally diverse symptoms can extend to the feeling that one is:
'being haunted by ghosts' (4).

In "...some cultural contexts; such as Native American communities and Cambodia, foster beliefs about spiritual importance of nightmares" (5a).

Culturally agreed understanding/concepts of trauma within communities can affect the presentation of the trauma symptomatology.

So too, religious and spiritual beliefs; and, utilisation of natural healing remedies, impact expressions of PTSD symptoms.

Consequently, this can create challenges in the understanding of cultural background and beliefs in the diagnosis of PTSD.

Thus, in the cross cultural context in particular, much relies on **efficient diagnosis** from specialised trauma clinicians, as some symptoms may be minimised, or remain unrecognised, otherwise.

Historical knowledge of the trauma, too, is vital for effective assessment and diagnosis.

"For example, people of Latino descent in the United States have been shown to be more vulnerable to PTSD following exposure to trauma than members of other ethnic groups; one potential explanation is that the cultural script of *ataque ne nervios* facilitates experience of symptoms consistent with PTSD" (5a).

In contrast, Germans (political prisoners of the GDR) post-release PTSD response process, typically occurred in the following ways: from 'fear' then to 'brokenness' then to the feeling of having had a 'stolen life'. There were minimal physical symptoms described and a reluctance to report dissociative symptoms (only referred to as 'spacing out') (5).

Please see page 28 for Cultural assessment information.

CPTSD: COMPLEX POST-TRAUMATIC STRESS DISORDER

Is featured in the **ICD-11**, with the following diagnostic criteria (2):

<u>6 symptom clusters:</u>

That is,

3 PTSD criteria (Re-experiencing trauma; Avoidance of trauma reminders; heightened sense of threat: hypervigilance, startle response)

3 disturbances of self organisation (**DSO**) (emotional dysregulation, interpersonal difficulties and negative self-concept).

Plus, **significant dysfunction** in one or more than 1 primary area of life functioning.

-**The 3 DSO categories are the deciding factor for CPTSD versus PTSD diagnosis**

-**All** (of the above) diagnostic criteria above must be satisfied.

-Exposure to **at least 1** traumatic event (witnessed/ experienced).

-The traumatic event must have been **extremely threatening or horrific.**

-**Cannot** be diagnosed with PTSD and CPTSD, must be either one, or the other.

-Eg sufferers: child abuse histories.

-**Differential diagnosis**: borderline personality disorder; major depressive disorder.

-Medical problems are inclusive often in CPTSD.

-Incorporates children and young people.

Flashbacks:

-sudden, intrusive memories;

-loss of awareness of current surroundings;

-loss of sense of time;

-physical and emotional responses (eg fight or flight reaction);

-sensory features;

-reliving the trauma to the point that the victim involuntarily, during flashbacks, undertakes eg. verbalisations of parts of the traumatic incident (eg help).

Dissociative fugue (can be linked with depersonalization; dissociative identity disorder):

-loss of autobiographical information;

-in extreme cases starting a new life; a type of reversible amnesia.

TRIGGERS' examples: television programmes (eg similar stories, facial features etc); being touched; specific sounds; similar voices.

CPTSD: AVOIDANCE OF TRAUMA REMINDERS

-Goes above and beyond evading discussion of trauma to ***avoiding all*** potential triggers.

-Changes in lifestyle, and habits.

-Can involve obsessive-compulsive cognitions (fears) and new behaviors to reinforce the avoidance.

-Avoidance of environments.

For instance, in ***MVA trauma:*** avoidance of streets, suburbs; driving, itself; travelling as a passenger in a car.

For example, in ***sexual assault:*** avoidance of intimate relations; overwashing body, or alternative to this.

CPTSD. HEIGHTENED SENSE OF THREAT

(Hypervigilance; Exaggerated, or reduced, startle response)

-*Constant,* adrenalised alert to current sensory information and trauma triggers.

-*Heightened* sense of awareness to everything around the sufferer.

-Sensory overload.

-Extreme anxiety behaviors.

-Jumpy at even the smallest of sounds and movements.

-Interpreting everything in the traumatic experience.

-Interspersed with avoidance of places, situations and people.

-Fight or flight response.

CPTSD: EMOTIONAL DYSREGULATION

-*Inability* to calm self or, reduce anxiety.

-Emotionally labile/emotional lability, mood swings.

-Anger to anxiety to depression to irritability and temper tantrums and hyperactivity.

-*Extreme* displays of emotion.

-Can be suffered by adults and children.

-Considered as behaving very immaturely in non-traumatised adult populations.

-Poor impulse control.

-Can manifest in overeating, binge drinking, insomnia, addiction problems, and *self-harm*.

-Sufferers often have a history of childhood sexual abuse.

-Affects levels of concentration.

-Difficulty **relating with others** who are not aware of/ had witnessed/ experienced the traumatic incident.

-So involved in the constantly relived trauma experience, that it leaves **little time to interact** with others, about daily events and other aspects of life.

-Live in their **'own world'**.

CPTSD: NEGATIVE SELF-CONCEPT

-Very poor/low self-esteem.

-Very low self-confidence in **decision making, intuition** and often questioning of one's own **sanity**.

-Feeling of incapability/ damaged to the **point of no return**.

-Feeling that everyone can see the traumatisation, or can sense that the sufferer is a trauma victim and unable to cope.

-affects all areas of life:

work,

relationships (including with loved ones who had been in their lives prior to the traumatic incident: husband/wife, children, siblings, grandchildren).

SVS: Second Victim Syndrome, and Second Victim Phenomenon

The first victim of a healthcare adverse event or medical error is naturally the patient (secondarily are the patients' family and carers).

'Second victims' (6) are: healthcare employees who were involved in an unexpected medical error and/or an adverse healthcare event which resulted in patient harm.

Second Victim Syndrome is described as:

"Second victims may display similar emotions and behaviors to those who are experiencing burnout. Providers may experience emotional lability, isolation, a decreased ability to focus, and may withdraw themselves from their support networks" (7).

Stages of second victim syndrome (8):

stage 1. *chaos and accident response*

stage 2. *intrusive reflections*

stage 3. *restoring personal integrity*

stage 4. *enduring the inquisition*

stage 5. *obtaining emotional first-aid*

stage 6. *moving on*

stage 4 is the most crucial to access support mechanisms (otherwise, the trauma may become long-lasting), as it involves potential consequences for the SVS sufferer's actions related to the medical error/critical healthcare incident.

ASD: Acute Stress Disorder: Assessment

<u>The National Stressful Events Survey Acute Stress Disorder Scale (NSESSS-ASD):</u>

Is utilised post-initial diagnosis of ASD, and to monitor changes in symptom severity (can be used as an assessment tool during treatment).

It is a 7 item scale.

The NSESSS-ASD measures ASD severity of symptoms (9a).

<u>Acute Stress Disorder Scale (ASDS-12):</u>

As with several other scales, physicians (in addition to Psychologists and other appropriate allied health staff) can use the Acute Stress Disorder Scale (9b).

-self-administered

-14-items scale.

-It is based on *DSM-5 (relevance with DSM-5-TR)* criteria.

-Assesses for ASD.

-Helps predict potential for development of PTSD.

-Focus of scale encompasses the ***primary elements*** of ASD and PTSD criteria.

<u>*Impact of Events Scale- Revised (IES-R):*</u>

Though *not used typically* as a primary diagnostic tool for diagnosis of *PTSD*.

It is a highly effective tool to measure **post-trauma phenomena.**

Useful in particular, to identify **hyperarousal symptoms** of ASD and PTSD.

It assesses the *extent* of distress the trauma victim is experiencing in response to the traumatic incident/s.

The IES-R **evaluates symptoms** such as:

-reminders of trauma;

-insomnia;

-anger;

-avoidance;

-triggered memories;

-hypervigilance;

-numbing;

-flashbacks;

-nausea,

-heart pounding,

-sweating,

-breathing problems;

-dreams;

-and hypervigilance (10).

The **STAXI-2; DASS; BAI; BDI-II;** and **BHS** (listed below) are all relevant for use for specific symptoms of ASD, once the diagnosis of ASD has been made.

This will assist in developing focussed responses to specific problematic symptoms.

PTSD: Post-Traumatic Stress Disorder: Assessment

Assessment, for presenting trauma symptomatology, and for differential diagnosis:

<u>**_Clinician Administered Post-Traumatic Stress Disorder Scale (CAPS-5):_**</u>

This is considered the 'gold standard' for PTSD assessment- consistent with DSM-5 (and with continued relevance with DSM-TR) criteria.

It is a 30-item structured interview.

It assesses **onset** of PTSD symptoms, and length of **symptom duration**.

Testing time: approximately, 45 to 60 minutes.

There are **3 different versions** of CAPS-5 (assessment for PTSD: in the past week; past month; and, lifetime PTSD).

The LEC-5 (The Life Events Checklist for DSM-5) is recommended as an accompaniment to CAPS-5.

Administration of CAPS-5 can be undertaken "by clinicians and clinical researchers who have a working knowledge of PTSD but can also be administered by appropriately trained paraprofessionals" (5b).

<u>***Post-Traumatic Stress Disorder Checklist- 5 (PCL-5).***</u>

Is utilised for **provisional diagnosis** of PTSD, and also to **monitor** for improvements/ deteriorations during treatment.

The scale has **3 versions**, including one with which the LEC-5 is to accompany.

The PCL-5 is a 20 point self-report questionnaire

-**encompassing issues** with:

memory; dreams; stress triggers;

physical reactions (heart, breathing, sweating);

trauma- activity and discussion- avoidance;

social distancing; apathy; pending doom;

insomnia; anger; hypervigilance;

poor concentration; and anger (5c).

<u>***The Mini International Neuropsychiatric Interview (M.I.N.I- 7.0.2):***</u>

Is brief (15 minutes) to administer, is used in **psychiatric evaluation, as well as by many different types of mental health professionals worldwide.**

-It has been converted into 70 different languages.

-The original M.I.N.I assesses for the arguably **most common** mental health disorders, that is, **17** in total.

For instance:

-post-traumatic stress disorder;

-major depressive disorder;

-suicidality;

-mania and bipolar disorders;

-panic disorder; agoraphobia; anxiety disorders;

-obsessive-compulsive disorder;

-substance use disorders;

-some psychotic features;

-eating disorders;

-anti-social personality disorder (12).

___

Post-Traumatic Stress Diagnostic Scale (PDS-5):

-It is a self-administered test, it has 24 items.

-It takes approximately 15 minutes to complete.

-The PDS is applicable for ***13 years and older*** literacy levels.

-Is used both as a ***screening tool*** for PTSD of persons who report having suffered a traumatic event, as well as ***assessing for severity*** of PTSD symptoms over the last month period, and examines the onset of the symptoms suffered.

-The scale includes assessment of: confirmation of trauma type; extent of response; and *DSM-5* (relevance with DSM-5-TR) criteria for PTSD (13).

___

BAI (anxiety): Beck Anxiety Inventory:

-It is a 24 point scale.

-Is self-administered.

-Likewise with the BDS, and BHS, the length of administration time is brief.

-21 common symptoms of anxiety are evaluated.

-The inventory is available in numerous languages (14)

**BDI-II (depression): Beck Depression Inventory-II:**

**It measures the:**

-physiological;

-cognitive;

-affective;

-motivation

elements of depression (15).

**BHS (hopelessness): Beck Hopelessness Scale:**

-It is **often used** effectively with the **BDI-II.**

-Requires the choice of true or false responses.

-It has 20 points.

-The BHS assists in **assessing suicidal ideation** along with **levels of hopefulness**.

-Assesses loss of motivation, feelings about one's future, and expectations (16)

__DASS (depression and anxiety): Depression Anxiety and Stress Scale__

-different versions available: 8; 12; 21 items

Assesses for:

-Physical symptoms: panic; heart rate

"The depression scale assesses dysphoria, hopelessness, devaluation of life, self-deprecation, lack of interest/involvement, anhedonia and inertia. The anxiety scale assesses anxiety, and subjective experience of anxious affect. The stress scale is sensitive to levels of chronic non-specific arousal. It assesses difficulty relaxing, nervous arousal, and being easily upset/agitated, irritable/over-reactive and impatient." (17).

Assessment of Cultural Factors

<u>The cultural formulation interview for the DSM-5-TR</u>

Assists in understanding cultural contexts, for instance- in the traumatised individual.

It *defines culture in multitudinous ways.*

The interview examines areas such as:

-social supports;

-resiliency;

-capacity of personal resources.

It has *3* sections, the *first* (a 16 question interview), including the following *4 domains*:

Cultural definition of the problem;

Cultural perception of cause, context and support;

Cultural factors affecting self-coping and past help-seeking;

Cultural factors affecting current help seeking.

The *second* section involves evaluation of perspectives of persons related to the patient/ client.

The *third* section incorporates supplementary information acquired based on the first sections' (above) domains (18; 1).

CPTSD: Complex Post-Traumatic Stress Disorder: Assessment

In addition to the entries (above listed) in the PTSD assessment categories, the following is relevant:

International Trauma Questionnaire (ITQ):

-This has been ***specifically developed for diagnosis of CPTSD.***

-Is consistent with ICD-11 criteria.

-It is an 18 item scale.

-Which is self-administered.

-It assists in evaluating the ***primary elements*** related to PTSD and CPTSD (19).

State-Trait Anger Expression Inventory- 2 (STAXI-2)

-This has 57 items.

-It can be administered by numerous different workers.

-The interpretation of scores, however, ideally needs to be undertaken by a healthcare worker trained in psychology, or psychiatry.

-It has interpretative software available in several languages.

The **STAXI-2 subscales** include:

-State anger;

-Trait anger;

-Anger expression-out;

-Anger expression- in;

-Anger control- out;

-Anger control-in;

-Anger expression index (20).

It can be used for trauma related **emotional dysregulation** to consideration of effects on **medical conditions** through to assessment of *forensic populations*.

SVS: Second Victim Syndrome: Assessment

Second Victim Experience and Support Tool (SVEST):

Developed specifically for **healthcare employees** who have been involved in a healthcare **adverse event**.

It has 7 dimensions:

-psychological distress;

-physical distress;

-colleague support;

-supervisor support;

-institutional support;

-non-work-related support;

-professional self-efficacy.

Additionally, the SVEST can aid in the examination of **degree of absenteeism** and level of **commitment** to work post-diagnosis of Second Victim Syndrome (21).

<u>*Maslach Burnout Inventory (MBI):*</u>

In order to cater for ***differential diagnosis*** of (for instance) burnout, the following scale is helpful:

MBI-HSS (MP): Maslach Burnout Inventory Human Services Survey for Medical Personnel

It has 22 items within the inventory.

3 scales:

-emotional exhaustion;

-depersonalization;

-personal accomplishment.

MBI-HSS: Maslach Burnout Inventory-Human Services Survey can include nurses, physicians, allied health and, police.

It has the 3 scales (as above).

The brief questionnaire: **AWS (Areas of Worklife Survey)** is a recommended tool to accompany the MBI it measures perceptions to examine work engagement and burnout (22).

CASE SCENARIOS:
Please preliminarily diagnose these trauma case victims..
ASD; PTSD; CPTSD; or SVS

Case 1: Helena

Which preliminary diagnosis fits best; what are the reasons for your answer; please discuss:

Case 1: Helena

- 40 year old female

-lived in a rural area her entire life

-male partner/perpetrator owns many guns

-she has suffered severe domestic violence (for multiple years), including a history of the partner having broken the victim's jaw

-Helena/victim has a child to the perpertrator

-rural police know the perpetrator as friends

-the victim fled with her son and no belongings to the city

-Helena's friends in the rural area were sworn to secrecy regarding her's and her son's new living arrangements

-1 month after the move she receives more death threats as the perpetrator had discovered her whereabouts in the city

-her car was subsequently set fire to

-the perpetrator/father turned up to her child's school and attempted to abduct the child

-the victim feared for her's and her son's life, everyday

-the perpetrator attempted murder of Helena, by shotgun, 1 week ago

-city law enforcement personnel were not interested in her reported concerns until the shotgun incident, as the origins of the DV were 'out of area'

-one week following the attempted murder, Helena presents to emergency with: *uncontrollable shaking; she cannot recall ever feeling so anxious and terrified before; she describes her heart pounding and difficulty breathing; she cannot stop thinking about the harm done by the perpetrator; she is very negative about her's and her son's future; and does not want to return to the house where the attempted murder occurred.*

-*the emergency staff diagnose the patient with traumatic shock.*

(This is often a standard story of DV in many regions)

a) CPTSD

b) PTSD

c) ASD

d) SVS

e) none of the above

Case 2: Keeva

Which preliminary diagnosis fits best; what are the reasons for your answer; please discuss:

Case 2: Keeva

-45 years old

-lives in an urban area

-her husband/perpetrator is a member of a gang

-Keeva/victim (wife) was kept prisoner for several years by her husband/perpetrator

-relatives all around her are also in a gang

-other gang members have a history of stalking the victim and reporting back to the perpetrator

- the victim sought counselling but remained with the perpetrator (out of fear for safety and life)

-many undisclosed horrific things have been witnessed by Keeva as part of the perpetrator's gang activities

-6 months ago, the victim fled to a women's refuge but her husband perpetrated violence upon several of the refuge workers and other women staying in the refuge, the victim thus returned home

Keeva is very jumpy and anxious; she constantly relives the traumatic memories; feels she is doomed; has outbursts of anger; and perspires alot.

NB: in multiple Western regions, much of the time the perpetrator easily discovers in which refuge the victim is housed, within hours

a) PTSD

b) SVS

c) ASD

d) CPTSD

e) none of the above

Case 3: Tepiora

Which preliminary diagnosis fits best; what are the reasons for your answer; please discuss:

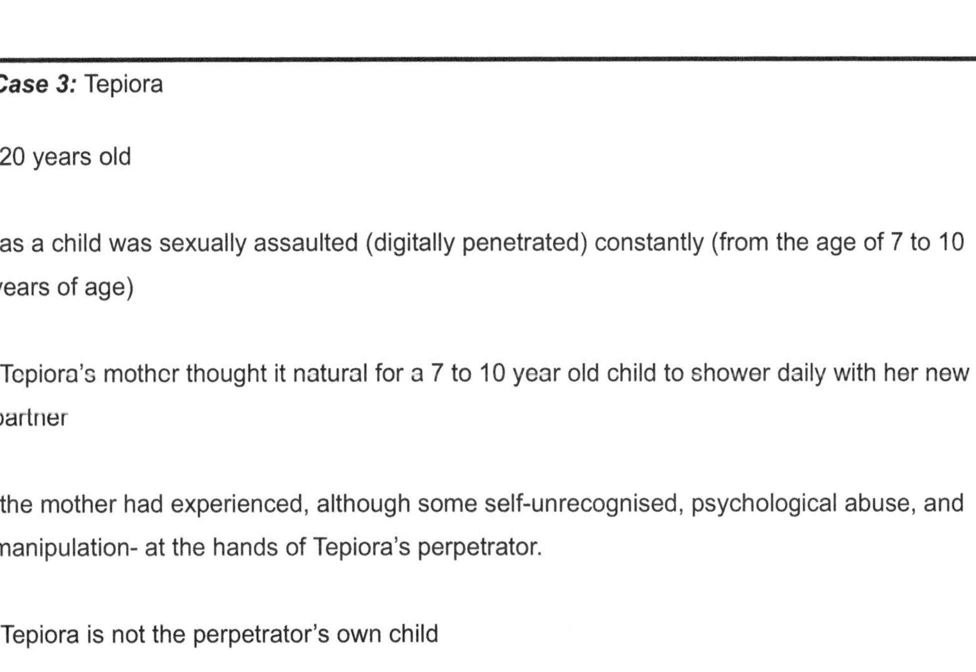

Case 3: Tepiora

-20 years old

-as a child was sexually assaulted (digitally penetrated) constantly (from the age of 7 to 10 years of age)

-Tepiora's mother thought it natural for a 7 to 10 year old child to shower daily with her new partner

-the mother had experienced, although some self-unrecognised, psychological abuse, and manipulation- at the hands of Tepiora's perpetrator.

-Tepiora is not the perpetrator's own child

-Tepiora is regularly told by her siblings that she behaves like a child; she does not ever recall being childlike but because she does not believe that she has positive qualities she doubts her own judgement about perceptions; the victim lives alone and self-isolates to avoid feeling threatened; the victim has compulsions like checking locked doors, and bathing 4 times per day.

a) ASD

b) PTSD

c) CPTSD

d) SVS

e) none of the above

Case 4: Ela

Which preliminary diagnosis fits best; what are the reasons for your answer; please discuss:

Case 4: Ela

-14 years old

-the victim was raped and molested from the age of 3 yo to 13 yo by her natural/biological father

-the perpetrations occured always in the early hours of the morning

-Ela's mother is a healthcare worker who worked from the early hours of the morning, 3 days per week

-the perpetrator/father had his own office adjacent to the house (open and readily accessible to all family members, including capability of witnessing by wife) where he would view and share extensive child pornography online

-he also placed the perpetration of his own child's sexual abuse upon a series of online websites

-in a rare event for this type of case, the perpetrator was gaoled for more than 10 yrs in a maximum penitentiary prison, for his crimes

-the mother was raising her children in a sect-like religion

-Ela had sought refuge (in same house) with siblings, immediately before the assaults took place, to no avail

-the victim had sought help (to no avail) from elders of sect-like religious church

-she had overseas relatives which she was helping to support via her healthcare work income and via her husband's/perpetrator's wages

-Ela's mother was involved in a critical incident at work, involving a patient who suffered an iatrogenic/ hospital induced life threatening event. The mother, as a healthcare worker, became very stressed, suffered from daily ruminations about the incident for a period of 4 weeks

-Ela presents with the following:
her school work has long suffered; she has lost many friendships; the entire family was displaced post-prison sentence of father/perpetrator; is considerably numbed about the events which had occurred; appears vague and unable to communicate for several minutes, on multiple occasions, when talking about the trauma suffered; she suffers from frequent nightmares and gasps/stops breathing during trauma based discussions. All in all she evades talking about the traumatic events, though she had been exposed to a lengthy court process.

For Ela:	For mother:
a) PTSD	a) SVS
b) CPTSD	b) CPTSD
c) SVS	c) PTSD
d) ASD	d) ASD
e) none of the above	e) none of the above

CASE 5: Birdie

Which preliminary diagnosis fits best; what are the reasons for your answer; please discuss:

Case 5: Birdie

-49 years old

-Birdie was raped by a very large man (with an IQ of 90) at the age of 11 years

-she was not the only victim perpetrated upon- others did not formally come forward- but told related family members

-The incident occurred in the following context:

    -the victim was at a 200 fold family celebration

    -Birdie was a direct relative of the perpetrator

    -she was encouraged to sit on her own, outside the house (adjacent to the perpetrator's room) by the perpetrator's mother

-with a wink, and a suggestive voice, the perpetrator invited the victim in to his room for a 'cup of coffee', that it 'would not hurt' her, 'I promise', whilst laughing and stating that 'it will taste really good'
(in the country where this occurred code for cup of coffee 'coc' means highly sexually suggestive intent and actions)

-the entire family network were of fundamentalist religious beliefs (so coffee was not allowed until a child/adolescent was at least 16 or 18 years of age)

-the victim innocently agreed to enter his room

-the brother of the perpetrator encouraged the victim into the perpetrator's singular room, attached to the family property

-another family member witnessed the grooming behaviors/proposition (cup of coffee etc), and informed a family member post-haste

-the mother of the perpetrator never accepted the victims' allegations

-upon the victim's disclosure, a huge family rift occurred

-there was at least 1 other victim of the same age who had been sexually perpetrated upon by the same perpetrator

-several months later, the perpetrator suddenly died, in an accident.

-a further rift emerged within the family, with the mother of the perpetrator (despite her direct knowledge and connection- familially- with the victims and the primary and secondary witnesses, who revealed all) used a 'prop' from her deceased son for at least 20 years in front of approximately 150 family members to illustrate the point that he/the perpetrator was an 'angel' and nothing less

-this continued on a grandscale at 6 monthly (and daily to weekly for direct family members) to yearly intervals in front of the victims- during family celebrations, and beyond- and all the way to her imminent demise

-for decades, aside from inside the immediate family circle, all remained silent about the abuse, the perpetrator's subsequent death, and the consequential reaction by the mother to the allegations.

-Birdie presents with the following:
mistrust and avoidance of all males; constant intrusive memories of the traumatic incident; difficulty calming herself when angry, anxious, and saddened; challenges with perceiving herself as anything other than an outcast;

very hyperalert about threats to safety and carries self-protection devices with her at all times; and has felt like this for a period of many years.

a) SVS

b) PTSD

c) CPTSD

d) ASD

e) none of the above

Treatment of ASD; PTSD; CPTSD; and SVS

<u>Treatment of ASD:</u>

-Physicians, or other healthcare practitioners, can **reinforce** the patient's **coping mechanisms**, including information about natural stress responses, minimisation of anxiety, and social/other support systems.

Then, where necessary, **refer** the patient to a psychologist, or psychiatrist.

-Critical incident debriefing (where appropriate).

-Trauma focussed CBT (TFCBT).

-Acceptance and Commitment therapy (ACT).

-Psychotherapeutic interventions (especially if the person has a history of previous trauma).

-Workplace programs/counsellor/debriefer/employment assistance program referral or Outsourcing for external psychological support.

-Both are perceived to assist in **minimising** workplace/workers' compensation claims, or workplace liability.

<u>**Treatment of PTSD:**</u>

-Debriefing.

-Exposure therapy.

-CBT.

-TFCBT.

-Psychotherapy.

-(Hypnosis & EMDR are ***highly controversial*** treatments, especially if the traumatic incident/s suffered comes to legal proceedings: can affect trauma memory, etc).

Treatment CPTSD:

-Per symptom.

-No specific overall model of treatment.

Suggested:

-Several of the PTSD therapeutic interventions, abovementioned, specifically:

-TFCBT

-EMDR: NB: must have great consideration before undertaking.

Treatment CPTSD Re-experiencing trauma:

-Exposure therapy.

-Grounding techniques.

-Identification of triggers.

<u>**Treatment CPTSD Avoidance of trauma triggers:**</u>

-Debriefing.

-Trauma counselling.

-Identification, and awareness of triggers.

-Exposure therapy.

-Narrative therapy.

<u>**Treatment CPTSD Heightened sense of threat:**</u>

-Biofeedback.

-Anxiety reduction techniques.

-CBT.

-Sometimes physicians, including psychiatrists, will prescribe anxiolytics.

<u>**Treatment CPTSD Emotional Dysregulation:**</u>

-DBT (dialectical behavior therapy). Could be useful ***in some instances***. For instance:
    challenging catastrophising

    involves CBT;

    Mindfulness;

    Psycho-educational, eg specific labelling of emotions.

-Positive reinforcement of structure.

-Mindfulness.

-TFCBT.

<u>**Treatment CPTSD Interpersonal difficulties:**</u>

-Trauma groups (with victims having suffered similar traumatic experiences).

-Re-building social supports.

-Providing educational information on CPTSD.

-CPTSD education for ***traumatised persons' loved ones*** (and sometimes where victim is agreeable, inclusion in some counselling sessions).

<u>Treatment CPTSD Negative self-concept:</u>

-Psychotherapy.

-Mindfulness.

-Self-esteem retraining.

<u>**Treatment SVS:**</u>

-Debriefing.

-Counselling support.

-Mentoring.

-Tiered support programmes (involving peers, and allied healthcare staff support or referrals).

-***Once multi-symptom trauma is identified***, use of ASD (and then PTSD where relevant) treatment tools are recommended.

Reporting risks

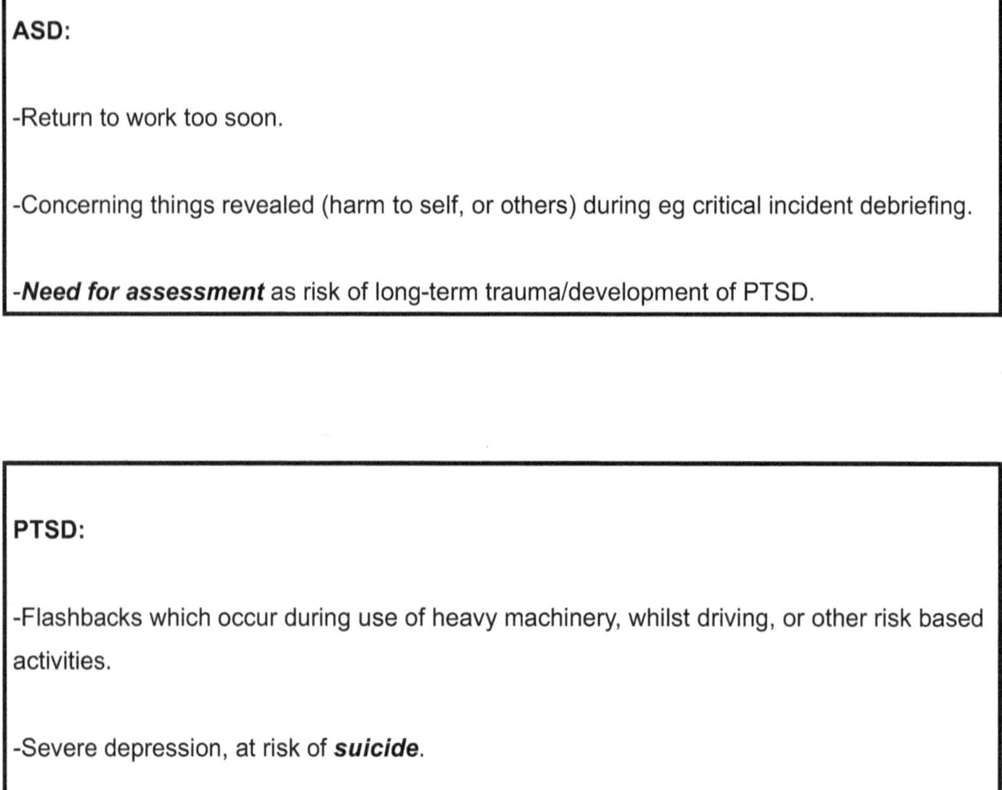

ASD:

-Return to work too soon.

-Concerning things revealed (harm to self, or others) during eg critical incident debriefing.

-***Need for assessment*** as risk of long-term trauma/development of PTSD.

PTSD:

-Flashbacks which occur during use of heavy machinery, whilst driving, or other risk based activities.

-Severe depression, at risk of ***suicide***.

-Misuse of anti-depressant medication, or anxiolytics.

-Substance abuse which is placing self, or others, at ***serious harm***.

-Vengeful feelings which extend beyond the usual anger expressed about the perpetrator/s (eg perturbation, planned use of weapon, aware of perpetrator's whereabouts, and has already initiated stalking behaviors).

CPTSD:

-Similarly with ASD and PTSD

-However, the effects of significant difficulties with emotional dysregulation can predispose the sufferer to aggressive outbursts, or extremes of other emotions.

This can cause vulnerability to family members, work colleagues, and strangers, alike especially if they are combined (or a result of) flashbacks (where the sufferer loses context of time and location).

Self-directed anger, and ***suicidal***: ideation, perturbation and attempt, are also at issue.

SVS:

-Clinical dysfunctionality.

-Risk of further ***medical errors***.

-Absenteeism, job/task refusal, quitting job.

-Risk of ***self-harm***.

-Avoidance of ***triggers*** which are commonplace in the workplace (syringes, medical monitoring equipment, specific categories of patients).

Limited Resources and Accessability to Support

Resource provision can be enhanced by:

-Self-help groups

-Localized education campaigns (eg pamphlets) and other resources, in doctor's offices, hospitals,etc

-Acknowledging that **ASD, PTSD, CPTSD** and **SVS** are both physical and psychological in nature

-Social media: **ASD, PTSD, CPTSD** and **SVS** with links to supportive and educational sites

-High risk workplaces eg banks; drivers; transporters; etc

-Increased awareness of, and workplace contracts with **EAP** (Employment Assistance Programme) type programmes to target victim support immediately (individual and group critical incident debriefing; referral for counselling)

-Victim support programmes mainstreamed

-Witness assistance accessability via police, emergency services (even if it is only a hotline).
Integrated procedure (information provision) as part of crime scene attendance, or upon victim reporting/ providing police statements; as part of court support processes

-Volunteers to assist in witness protection

-Dissemination of resources to physician and health educators/promotion with contact numbers or site access for advice.

AMBULANCE, POLICE, OTHER EMERGENCY PERSONNEL, INVOLVEMENT

The victim of a serious traumatic incident requires support in a number of ways.

This begins, and continues, with the need for:

Police:

-Enforcement of AVOs, domestic violence **orders**

-Taking of victim statements at the time (where appropriate, regarding the assault)

-Forwarding of victim statements to the appropriate office (district attorney, department of public prosecutions)

-Obligatory court support, giving statements on the victim's behalf, victim support

-**Contact** with relevant authorities/chains of command if perpetrator is attempting to engage police in discussion regarding the origin of the injuries incurred.

Ambulance officers, Paramedics:

-Where appropriate, taking of photographs of injuries/encouraging hospital staff to

-Contact with **police** if on-site help provided

-Full statements provided, as may be needed in court later

-Initial injuries documented fully, naturally (as with all involved):

-Without presupposition nor bias

-**Contact** with relevant authorities if perpetrator is attempting to engage ambulance personnel in discussion regarding the origin of the injuries incurred

-Key staff/representative personnel who can help with above processes to free ambulance officers up for other duties.

Other supportive emergency personnel who attend (instead of/concomitant with ambulance and police personnel):

-Full documentation necessary, even if requiring guidance regarding medical terminology and law enforcement related terms (seek support accordingly)

-Likewise with ambulance officers and police, verbalised information not just to be 'left with' emergency hospital workers and thence, departing in the case of the traumatised victim. Otherwise, this may place all at risk.

It is highly acknowledged that the above is dependant upon funding resources and availability of personnel to achieve the tasks at hand.

However, one can never tell when one is required (later) in the court/tribunal process regarding a case, so it is very necessary to dot every 'i' and cross every 't', for peace of mind.

Thereto, emergency personnel, police, and ambulance officers, are not expected to know every sub-clause of the country's nor state's legal processes, and how impossible legal cases can turn to possible ones, in due course.

ABBREVIATIONS; EXPLANATIONS

ACT: Acceptance and Commitment Therapy

ASD: Acute Stress Disorder

AVO: Apprehended Violence Order

CBT: Cognitive Behavioral Therapy

CPTSD: Complex Post-Traumatic Stress Disorder

DSM-5-TR (DSM-5 and DSM-IV): Diagnostic and Statistical Manual of Mental Disorders-5-TR (5 and IV)

DV: Domestic Violence

EAP: Employment Assistance Programme

EMDR: Eye Movement Desensitization and Reprocessing

GDR: German Democratic Republic (East Germany: 1949 to 1990)

HCPs: Healthcare Professionals

ICD-11 (and ICD-10): International Statistical Classification of Diseases and Related Health Problems-11 (and 10)

MVA: Motor Vehicle Accident

PTSD: Post-Traumatic Stress Disorder

SVS: Second Victim Syndrome

TFCBT: Trauma Focussed Cognitive Behavioral Therapy

REFERENCES

(1) American Psychiatric Association (2022), Diagnostic and Statistical Manual of
Mental Disorders, 5 th ed. Text Revision: DSM-5-TR. Washington, D.C.: American Psychiatric
Association Publishing.

(2) World Health Organization (2019), International Statistical Classification of Diseases and
Related Health Problems, 11th ed,; ICD-11.

(3) Gilmoor, A.R., Adithy, A. and Regeer, B. The cross-cultural validity of post-traumatic stress
disorder and post-traumatic stress symptoms in the Indian context: a systematic search and
review. Frontiers in Psychiatry. July 2019, 10, Article 439. www.frontiersin.org

(4) De Jong, J.T.V.M., Komproe, I.H., Van Ommeren, M., El Masri, M. Araya, M., Khaled, N., van
den Put, W. and Somasundaram, D. (2001). Lifetime events and posttraumatic stress disorder in 4
postconflict settings. JAMA 286, 555-562.0

(5a) Chentsova-Dutton, Y. and Maercker, A. Cultural scripts of traumatic stress: outline,
illustrations, and research opportunities. Frontiers in Psychology: hypothesis and theory, Nov 2019,
10, Article 2528. Luhrmann, T. (Ed.). www.frontiersin.org

(5b) PTSD: National Center for PTSD. VA>>Health Care>>PTSD: National Center for PTSD>>
US Department of Veteran Affairs Providers>>Assessment>>Clinician-Administered PTSD Scale
for DSM-5 (CAPS-5). www.ptsd.va.gov

(5c) Weathers, F.W., Litz, B.T., Keane, T.M., Palmieri, P.A., Marx, B.P. and Schnurr, P.P. (2013). The PTSD Checklist for DSM-5 (PCL-5). National Center for PTSD. www.ptsd.va.gov

(6) Wu, A.W. Medical error: The second victim. The doctor who makes the mistake needs help too. Br Med J. 2000; 320(7237):726-727.

(7) Tabatabai, R. and Pilarski, A. (2021). Second victim syndrome. In EMRA wellness guide section 8.:Chung, A.S. (Ed.). TX, USA: Emergency Medicine Residents' Association www.emra.org

(8) Scott, S.D., Hirschinger, L.E., Cox, K.R., McCoig, M., Brandt, J. and Hall, L.W. The natural history of recovery for the health care provider 'second victim' after adverse events. Qual Saf Health Care. 2009; 18(5):325-330.

(9a) Kilpatrick, D.G., Resnick, H.S. and Friedman, M.J. (2013). The National Stressful Events Survey Acute Stress Disorder Scale (NSESSS-ASD). Arlington: American Psychiatric Association.

(9b) Bryant, R.A., Harvey, A.G., Dang, S.T. and Sackville, T. Assessing acute stress disorder: psychometric properties of a structured clinical interview. Psychol. Assess. 1998; 10(3): 215-220.

(10) Weiss, D.S. (2007). The impact of event scale-revised. IN J.P. Wilson & T.M. Keane (Eds.) Assessing psychological trauma and PTSD: a practitioner's handbook (2nd ed., pp.168-169), NY:Guilford Press.

(11) Lang, A.J. and Stein, M.B. An abbreviated PTSD checklist for use as a screening instrument in primary care. Behav Res Ther. 2005 May; 43(5):589-94.

(12) Sheehan, D.V., Lecrubier, Y., Sheehan, K.H., Amorim, P., Janaus, J., Weiller, E., Hergueta, T., Baker, R. and Dunbar, G.C. (1998). The mini-international neuropsychiatric interview (M.I.N.I): The development and validation of a structured diagnostic psychiatric interview for DSM-IV and ICD-10. J Clin Psychiatry. 1998; 59 Suppl 20:22-33; quiz 34-57.

(13) Foa, E.B. The post-traumatic stress diagnostic scale manual. National computer systems inc., 1995.

(14) Beck, A.T. and Steer, R.A. (1993). Beck Anxiety Inventory Manual. San Antonio, TX: Psychological Corporation.

(15) Beck, A.T., Steer, R.A. and Brown, G.K. (1996). BDI-II: Beck depression inventory manual. 2nd edn. San Antonio, TX: Psychological Corporation.

(16) Beck, A.T. (1988). Beck hopelessness scale. San Antonio, TX: Psychological Corp. NY: Harcourt Brace Jovanovich.

(17) Livelihood, S.H. and Lovibond, P.F. (1995). Manual for the depression anxiety and stress scales. (2nd Ed.). Sydney: Psychology Foundation.

(18) APA (2013) Diagnostic and statistical manual of mental disorders 5th Ed (DSM-5) Handbook on the cultural formulation interview (CFI). Lewis-Fernandez, R., Aggarwal, N.K., Hinton, L., Hinton, D.E. and Kurmayer, L.J. (Eds). USA: American Psychiatric Association Publishing

(19) Cloitre, M., Sherlin, M., Brewin, C.R., Bisson, J.I., Roberts, N.P., Maercker, A., Karatzias, T. and Hyland, P. (2018). The international trauma questionnaire: Development of a self-report measure of ICD-11 PTSD and complex PTSD. Acta Psychiatrica Scandinavica.

(20) Spielberger, D.C. (1999). STAXI-2 state trait anger expression inventory-2, Professional manual. Florida: PAR.

(21) Burlison, J.D., Scott, S.D., Browne, E.K., Thompson, S.G. and Hoffman, J.M. The second victim experience and support tool (SVEST): Validation of an organizational resource for assessing second victim effects and the quality of support resources. J Patient Saf. 2017 Jun; 13(2):93-102.

(22) Maslach, C., Jackson, S.E., Leiter, P., Schaufeli, W.B. and Schwab, R.L. (2022). Maslach Burnout Inventory (MBI). www.mindgarden.com

Copyright ©. 2022. M.D. Tophus. All rights reserved.

www.ingramcontent.com/pod-product-compliance
Lightning Source LLC
Chambersburg PA
CBHW061018260726

48661CB00005B/2229